# Jesus–My Very Best Friend
## A BOOK ABOUT FRIENDSHIP

Ke
Illustrate

Chariot Books™ is an imprint of David C. Cook Publishing Co.
David C. Cook Publishing Co., Elgin, Illinois 60120
David C. Cook Publishing Co., Weston, Ontario
JESUS–MY VERY BEST FRIEND
© 1990 David C. Cook Publishing Co., Elgin, IL
Design by Dawn Lauck
All rights reserved.
First Printing, 1990. Printed in Hong Kong
95 94 93 92 91 90 5 4 3 2 1
ISBN 1-55513-306-1 LC 89-62118

The verse marked (TLB) is taken from *The Living Bible* ©1971,
owned by assignment by the Illinois Regional Bank N.A. (as trustee).
Used by permission of Tyndale House Publishers, Inc., Wheaton, IL
60189. All rights reserved.

If I went down in a submarine
till the starfish blinked
and the sun turned green,
way down deep in the deepest sea
I know who would be there with me—
Jesus, my very best friend!

If I decided to climb Pikes Peak
to hike for a day
or even a week
and the woods were dark and full of
    bears—
I'd talk to Jesus. I know He cares,
'cause He's my very best friend!

If I rode a rocket to the stars
to play on Pluto
or march on Mars
or chase a comet all over the place—
Jesus would be there. He made
   outer space
and He is my very best friend!

When I'm a pirate in a pirate suit,
with a pirate ship
and rich pirate loot,
and my sister asks if she can play,
I think to myself, what would Jesus
    say?
'Cause He's my very best friend!

I once threw a tantrum, a terrible fit,
and Mommy paddled
me right where I sit.
I was afraid I'd made Jesus sad.
I told Him "I'm sorry,"
that I had been bad,
AND . . .
He was STILL my very best friend!

I'd go to Portugal, Paris, or Spain
to meet all the children
so I could explain,
"There's someone who will be with you
wherever you are
whatever you do—
Jesus, YOUR very best friend!"

Jesus said,
"I am with you always,
even to the end of the world."
MATTHEW 28:20b
Taken from *The Illustrated Bible* (TLB)